My Home in the
Jungle

My Home in the Jungle

Diary of an Ex-pat

Neil A. Hoag

To order additional copies of this book, contact:
Xlibris Corporation
1-888-795-4274
www.Xlibris.com
Orders@Xlibris.com
84636

DEDICATION

This book is dedicated to my wife, Marze Cabel Hoag, the love of my life, the inspiration to my words, the mother of my children, and owner of my heart. I pray that you are always beside me, and your faith moves me, and your beauty drives me. You're all the best things; you're my angel, my soul mate, my lover. You're the greatest thing in this world, a true inspiration from God, and God smiled on me on the day he you sent you to me. And I'm truly forever in your debt; you gave me direction, and that has changed my life forever, and you have humbled me, and you have made me wealthy beyond my dreams—all my wealth is being with you. So I dedicate this book to you.

Your soul mate,

Neil A. Hoag

nanay Luceta

tatay Benjamin

CHAPTER 1

INTRODUCTION

So here we go. My name is Neil A. Hoag. I'm the son of Neil S. Hoag and Karen Jenkins. I have two brothers, David and Steve, and a sister, Karen, as well. I was born in a small town in Southern Michigan in a rural farming community very far from neighbors, seven miles from the school we attended. Our childhood was one of little comforts, so we kept to ourselves. My father, a butcher, and my mother, a secretary at Albion College, did their best to give us a good life.

As a child, we had horses, and I learned to ride at a very young age. I had a small motorcycle when I was seventeen. I moved to Palm Beach, Florida. I worked at many various jobs by the time I was eighteen. I drove for a small taxi company that primarily served the Palm Beach island community, home of the rich and famous. And I would find work driving and serving wealthy families. I prided myself in being a great chauffeur and being able to separate myself from my work and deal with abstract personalities of the rich and famous and act professional.

By the time I was nineteen, I met my first wife, Diane. We were young and wild. I had a motorcycle, and we rode everywhere. We like to party beer and played pool. Broke a lot of rules. Made a lot of childish mistakes. Then by the time we turned twenty-three, May oldest son Kevin was born.

We finished college, and we moved to Germany, lived there for five years. Before we separated, I returned to the States, had to learn the single life once again, so I drove a taxi eighty hours a week.

I met a Filipina on a blind date set up by an old Filipina woman who got in the back of my taxi in West Palm Beach. She said that I seemed like a nice man, would I like a Filipina wife? I told her I had not given it any thought before. She said she knew a young lady, so I gave her my phone number. Two weeks later, I got a phone call from a girl saying her name was Meena, and we went on a date, and it was great. We hit it off beautifully. We had a great romance. After a few weeks, she told me she was returning to London, England, so I asked her if she wanted me to move to London, and she agreed, so I sold my things. I had a sports car, motorcycle, tools and got the ticket; I lived there for two years.

Her ex-husband found out she was involved with an American man, so he came to London to stop our relationship. He extorted her and told her he would take their daughter and she would never find her, so we both agreed that it would be best if I went back to America. My heart was broken. I was crushed; it was a very difficult time for me. So I started attending a Pentecostal church, and I prayed and looked for hope, and one day, while I was in prayer, I looked up and saw two pretty Filipinas sitting across from me, so I got my courage together and walked over and said hello. One of the girls responded to me. She was beautiful and had long curly hair and a nice body. We connected; we were inseparable. She had a warm and wonderful quality to her, and when we finally made love, it shook the house. We couldn't keep our hands off each other everywhere in every way known to man and a few positions that had never been discovered yet; we were pioneers of the sex world, and we became such good friends. We went everywhere together, and we always made each other happy. Even through bad times, we could always put a smile on each other's face. Then she moved to North Carolina, and we lost touch. I heard she remarried a member of the Billy Graham ministry and that she was happy, and I was happy for her.

So I continued driving a taxi. I started buying old limousines, first two then later three more, and started Beach Town Limousine. At first I put my cars at topless clubs; there were always problems with competing taxis and limos, so I put an ad on the paper, looking for drivers, and I got this call from a man who was looking for work, so I scheduled an interview. He was a gay man in his forties, and he suggested that I put my cars at gay clubs through South Florida, so I said why not, so I hired gay drivers, and the company started to make money, and we did well. He was sick with HIV infection, and before he died, I sold the company in 2001, and it was time to move on with my life. I wanted a fresh start; I didn't want to drive a taxi the rest of my days, so I went on vacation to visit my aunt.

December 2001 I went to Michigan to visit my aunt Vernie. She has a house on Duck Lake, and we had a great time; we played music, told stories, and she told me about her trip to the Philippines where she visited her brother. She showed me pictures, and I asked for his e-mail. And as soon as I returned to Florida, I sent a e-mail to him, and his wife responded, and I asked her if she could introduce me to a nice girl. And a couple weeks went by, and I got a letter in the mail.

She wrote me that she was twenty-two and a black beauty with long black hair; she told me she loved going to church and talking with her friends and that her mother and family were everything to her, so we wrote letters for almost a year; on her birthday, I sent her a crucifix and twenty dollars.

Her letters became so powerful to me. I would wait for the letters; those letters gave me hope and made me believe that love still existed on the planet. I was the happiest I'd ever been, and I hadn't even met her yet; her written words had power, and I've never felt alone since.

So I wrote her a letter, and I told her that I would come to the Philippines, and if we liked each other, we would take it from there, and she agreed; she was willing to wait, and all the relationships I had ever had were terrible, and I knew it wasn't going to cut it, so I was ready to start a new life.

I didn't have a clue on how things were gonna go down, but I figured with all that had happened to me so far, what the hell, I would take the chance and just go for it; it sounded like an adventure to me, so I got my affairs in order and got the plane ticket and rolled the dice. Even my closest friends tried to talk me out of it, saying they will kill me or I will get kidnapped, but my mind was made up, and I knew one was going to change my mind. I was on my way, and that was that, and I'm so glad that I didn't listen to them; they didn't know what they were talking about.

CHAPTER 2

FIRST TRIP TO THE PHILIPPINES

F light departed on August 7, 2002, arrived on August 9, 2002, 4:00 p.m. after flying almost twenty-three hours.

I got to Manila, then I found a flight going to Tacloban. The layover was six hours, but that didn't bother me, so I waited in the domestic terminal in Manila. There's a smoking room with glass doors, nicotine-stained yellow, and the walls were all smoked and stained, and an electric air-filter system, but it had seen its glory days a long time ago. The air was pungent with tobacco, and outside the smoke room was a shrine with Mother Mary, and there was a sign on the wall don't joke about bombs in the terminal eleven months after the planes flew into the trade towers.

So it's time to get on the plane and go to Tacloban, and they sat me next to a man in a turban, a Middle Eastern man, and I was the only white man on the plane, so we kept looking at each other through the corners of our eyes, and he was just as uncomfortable as I, but neither of us let our guard down during the flight. We arrived in Tacloban, Leyte, so I hopped on a taxi to the downtown market area and started to explore the market, and I noticed that everyone was staring at me, and three young girls were following me, so I gave them a few pesos, thinking they would go away. No such luck; fifteen minutes later, I had 120 kids following me. I could not move freely, so I had a panic attack, jumped in front of a bus, and hopped on a motorcycle taxi and told the driver to take me back to the airport.

When I got there, I picked a taxi driver who looked frail so if I had to kick his ass, I could take him easy; unfortunately, his car had issues, and he decided to stop at his house to show his family the American. He found it was odd, but I indulged him and said hello to his mother and father and met his sisters, and he said his sisters are single if I was interested in either one of them. I said no and we should get back on the road; I had been travelling for three days, and I knew I had to get to Southern Leyte.

We broke down seven times on the six-hour taxi ride to Southern Leyte. It was dark, and his car kept stalling, so he would turn off the lights and try to start the car, and buses would dodge around the car. At the last second, while I was praying in the back of this broken-down Toyota taxi, we kept asking people where's Malitbog. Finally, we found a young man who knew this barrio called Sangahon in the Municipality of Malitbog, so we arrived, and the whole village came out of their huts to see who the visitor was. I was at her house; her mother was there and asked one of her brothers to locate her. I gave her mother a kiss on the cheek; she turned red and went back into her house. Neighbors laughed. Finally, I met Marge. She asked me, "How was your trip?" I told her I had never been on a plane so long, so we sat on the front porch and talked for an hour, then she escorted me to the neighbor's house where I would sleep for the first few nights.

I could hear the grandmother talking through the night; her name is Austin. She is eighty-seven years old, and she got up, walked across the room where Marge, her friend Rolina, and Marge's brother Marrio were lying in the bed next to her, and she slapped Marrio with a stick on the butt. They all woke up and helped the old lady back to bed. But I was awake with jet lag, tossing and turning, thinking to myself, *What did I get myself into?* And so the morning sun came up so slowly; it was 6:00 a.m., and the house started to awake. Marge made me a

Nescafé, and we sat together and talked. She broke bread with me, and we shared a few things about ourselves.

Then we gathered my bags and walked to her mother's house on the other side of the village, and her mother was there, and she was so kind and thoughtful and invited me into the house, so I took off my sandals and entered the living room. The floors and walls were made of bamboo, and the old grass roof was rotted with holes. It humbled me, and she made me feel so welcome and so honored, so we dropped off my bags and continued on to the beach. And Marge's girlfriends were there.

We all sat at the beach and talked; the bay is so awesome, beautiful majestic. The bay is in a mountain cathedral; it's breathtaking, and Marge is beautiful and sweet and young, and she has such a nice outlook on life, and she has this personality that is very cool. She is just as her letters—kind, loving, willing, honest. She is breathtaking, the island girl of my dreams, not overly opinionated; she is sweet and graceful, not jaded or angry; in any capacity, she excites me to the bone. She is the woman I've been looking a lifetime for and I could have never found in America, and I feel happy that I made this trip.

So I took her and her friends out for breakfast. We joked and had a great time. I was not familiar with the smells in the third world or the sites, so I wanted to see everything. I was like a child the first time in a toy store, so captivated. Her girlfriends were all so pretty and nice; they asked me so many questions. For the first time I felt attractive and wanted, desired, and it was awesome. This is the way people are supposed to feel; I never felt this way being around American girls. And now I was sitting down at breakfast with six beautiful island girls who were competing for my affections; we laughed and joked and had a great time. We talked of our lives and childhoods, then we walked through town, and they were all hanging on to my every word.

They enjoyed speaking of their home and giggled at every opportunity, and they had questions, so I did my best to answer all of them.

Some of the questions were funny, like "Are there vampires in America?" I said, "No, but we have lots of lawyers, and they will suck the life out of you if given the opportunity." "What kinds of animals are in America?" And I told them "Lawyers," and one of them asked, "What is a lawyer?" But they didn't get my sense of humor, so I did my best to explain, and I used a mosquito as a reference, a blood sucker, a predator, a leech, an opportunist, a diablo.

Someone asked what I do for fun. I said to her I like visiting with old friends, drinking coffee with my close friend Mo; they asked me if he was single. I said yes, and the girls were all of a sudden more interested in Mo, then I said I have a friend named Brad. They asked, "Can you hook us up?" They all wanted a pen pal, so I told them that I would work on it.

CHAPTER 3

It was late August 2002. I was engaged to marry Marge Cabel, a Filipina girl from the Visayan islands. We were pen pals for over a year before I arrived, and we courted a month before we were engaged, so we moved into her aunt's (Yaya Dudi) house. It was a temporary arrangement devised by her family. Yaya Dudi had a two-room house made of concrete built by her son, so we stayed in her spare room.

It was an 8'×8' room with an old pipe-framed bed that was a hospital bed during WWII, with bamboo planks for a sleeping surface, no mattress, no foam, just bamboo.

The ceiling and walls were covered with geckos and other large lizards, and at night they were our entertainment. Through the night, I would always wake up hungry, so at night I would buy a piece of bread and put it on the bed stand, but when I would wake up, it was gone. I asked Marge in the morning if she ate the bread, and she didn't know why the bread disappeared every night.

I thought about it and figured that Dudi's grandchildren were taking the bread, so one night I got some fishing string, and I tied one end to the bread and the other end to a plastic Coke bottle and put the bottle on top of the door frame, hoping to catch the thief and bring this mystery to a close. So we fell asleep, and in the middle of the night, I heard the bottle fall, so I sprang from my bed, looked out the doorway; nobody was there, so I picked up the bottle and put it back above the doorway, and something struck the bottle out of my hands. I thought it was probably a gecko, so I tried again, and it hit the bottle even harder, so I got my matches off the bed stand, lit the match. There was a six-foot python on the top of the wall, coiled back and ready to strike, staring at me holding the match, so I fell back onto the bed, my head on Marge's belly.

She asked me what was wrong. I told her to look up, and we could see the silhouette of the snake; it wrapped itself around an old chandelier in the house, startled by my actions, so Marge called out to her aunt in the next room, and her aunt could see the snake. She called out "Jesus, Mary, and Joseph," waking up her grandchildren, got them up and into the kitchen. Marge ran and got her brother Jimmy. He had a machete. I found a six-foot bamboo, and we made a plan. I would get the snake down from the chandelier with the stick, and he would chop it. So I got the bamboo, and I was trying to get the snake down, but it's fighting with me. After a few minutes, finally the snake fell from the chandelier onto Dudi's bed. I got the bamboo under the snake and flung it into the living room. I jumped back to the living room and beat it to death with the bamboo stick until the bamboo stick I was holding was only ten inches long.

The room was filled with bamboo dust and debris. My hand was bleeding, and I wasn't sure if I was bitten by the snake, so Marge went and woke her uncle to ask "What should we do?" He said not to worry but don't drink any water. We finally went to sleep. It was 3:00 a.m. At 5:00 a.m. I woke to a large lizard falling on my chest from the ceiling. I was traumatized for a week afterward. I was victorious for defeating the serpent, and I'm not sure who took the bread off the bed stand or what, but shortly after that, we moved back to her mom's house.

After all that, my mother-in-law prepared snake cooked in coconut milk, and it was delicious, and we ate a lot of snakes after that, some as long as twenty feet, and I've killed many since. We prepare them like curry, boil them in coconut milk with hot peppers and ginger, and serve it over rice. It tastes like cinnamon with the texture of chicken; the ribs are very sharp, like needles after a strong typhoon. They come out of the mountains. Otherwise, they stay far away from man. They sometimes come to the village and eat a small pig or a chicken. Then they're helpless after they eat. Then you can pick them up or kill them with little or no threat.

CHAPTER 4

O ctober 28, 2002. Still have a bad ear infection, so Yaya Dudi insisted that I go to the witch doctor, so I agreed. So we rode in the multicab up the coast a little way then walked back into the jungle to a pig farm and there were lots of pigs; each pig had its own little cage made with rebar on a small concrete stage, very surreal, almost like a Salvador Dali painting. And lots of coconut trees there.

I could see an old woman working in the field, so she stopped working and came over and greeted us and invited us in to her house made of bamboo with a grass roof, so we entered her house. She had a cement floor, and children were staring at me through the wall and laughing. They don't see many white people in this part of the world, I understand, so she began with Nanay (Marge's mom). She started by saying a prayer and anointing her forehead with coconut oil, then she began to blow on the crown of her head while she's praying. Then she took a chicken egg and began to rub the unbroken egg over her forehead in a cross pattern, then she rubbed the egg down her arms, over her torso, down her back, with the belief that the egg will absorb the bad spirits and devils will be locked inside the egg. Then she wrapped the egg in a piece of tissue and gave it to Nanay and told her to take the egg home and throw it into the fire to destroy all the bad spirits, then she repeated this process with each of us, and when she was through, we asked her if she knew what was wrong with my ear. She said it was worms, then we asked her why Nanay was having shoulder pains. She has worms as well, so we said our good-byes and returned to Sangahon, me and my earache and three eggs to burn. I asked Marge if we could eat the eggs. She said no.

October 30, 2002. Returned to the witch doctor for a follow-up visit. This time I was asked to stare at a picture of Jesus, and she repeated the same process. Still an ear infection, so I told Marge that I wanted to eat the egg; she didn't see the humor in it. So at noon I went to Malitbog, to Dr. Chow's office. A fat doctor with no shirt and a stethoscope hanging around his neck examined me and prescribed amoxicillin for the ear infection. I told him I was already taking amoxicillin. He asked me if I enjoyed medicating myself. The office got quiet. I said I'm American, of course.

CHAPTER 5

SANGAHON

S angahon is a small village in the Municipality of Malitbog, where Marge's family came from. It was oddly named by the Japanese. It means "arch of the tree branch." During WWII, the Filipinos would hide in the large trees, and as the Japanese soldiers would come through, the Filipinos would hide in the arches of the large trees that extend back through into mountains.

The Japanese soldiers would yell "Sangahon," arch of the trees, referring to Filipinos hiding in the trees. That's how the village got its name, Sangahon, a jungle village.

Marge was born there and also her siblings. She had gone to school there as a child, so Marge has shared her history of events and took the time to teach me the genealogy of the village and her family tree that is very large. Marge's father fathered sixteen children, twelve children with Marge's mom. If anyone asks him about it, he tells them frankly "Chickens eat rice" as a reference to the nature of man. As of now, there are ten surviving children; half live in Cebu, half in Leyte.

Tatay was from a large family of eleven, and all his siblings had families of eight to ten children, so the immediate family is very large. The people are friendly and helpful in Sangahon. The children are well mannered and very pleasant to be around. They play games with their sandals on the street; it's like tag. Or they get these spiders and put them on a bamboo stick, and the spiders fight to the death; the kids bet on their spiders, like American kids play marbles. Or they play *lastiko*, a game with rubber bands. The children are well mannered here, and they give the elder people a bless—that's when you take the hand of an elder and put it to your forehead to show love and respect, and this applies to everyone in the community, including me. It's an exercise in honor to receive and to give a blessing.

The young guys in the village like to play basketball; the men gather into different groups and drink coconut wine (*tuba*), and they like to sing karaoke, and when you're walking through the village, a common greeting is "Asa man ka?" (Where are you going?), and the normal response is "Lakaw lakaw" (Walking, walking), "Salamat" (Thanks), or "Sari sari" (Wandering), "Sigi na" (Go), "Tana" (Come with me), "Gutom" (Hungry), "Busog" (Full), and "Taas elong" (Long nose).

In the evening, I like to walk through the village. Everyone, "Mayung gabi" (Good evening), and the men always offer me a drink of whatever they're having. The young girls flirt; some ask me, "Where are you going?" I say "Bukid" (mountains) or "Dagat" (beach), and I love these people.

Grandmothers taking care of little ones, people smiling and sharing with one another in good times and the bad, giving young people advice and sharing with them my life, the places I've been to, the stories of people in my taxi, my world of friends ten thousand miles away, sharing all the good and bad times. They always ask so many questions, and I love watching my children playing in the streets in a place where people live innocent lives and truly care for one another. I know in my heart that I picked the best place in the world to raise my children and have a wife who supports me emotionally and loves me unconditionally. She saved my life more than once; her commitment to me is unwavering, and her parenting skills surpass anything I've ever encountered in America.

The people of Sangahon are a part of me now; they are my sisters and brothers, nieces and nephews, cousins, aunts and uncles. They are my true wealth; they inspire me and protect me. We have shared the loss of family and friends together, and we have learned so much from one another and had wonderful days together. My coming to the jungle and living as the common people of the jungle has built a respect between me and the natives, so I write this book as a record of my migration to this tropical shore for my children and the future generations, as my greatest grandfather migrated to the American shores in 1635 and was given four Indian slave girls by David Lion Gardner of Gardner Island, and are family began in America. And this my children will share with their grandchildren.

As I've grown with these people in the jungle, they have changed me, and I believe I've changed them. To them I've always spoken of a world of possibility, that there's a big world out there, to seize the day, to take on challenges, and create the life that they truly want for themselves. I speak to them of the law of attraction, that anything is possible if you want it bad enough, to create a vision for themselves based on their vision of paradise and the things they truly want. Most people who come to Sangahon would see a poor third world village, and I've learned exactly the opposite. These people don't base their happiness on their possessions, but their true wealth is how they love one another and care for one another. If most Americans only knew we are a clueless culture on a treadmill, fighting for a life only to never feel true contentment in an over media-fed culture with all of its unhealthy distractions.

While I do love my country and have hopes for the future for America, we have created a path for ourselves that is unhealthy, and most of the people I meet tell me how hard things are and how difficult life is. They call to the universe for more of the same by the way they think. If you believe this life is difficult, then life will be difficult, but if you show gratitude in the things you do every day and take the time out to feel those feelings of true gratitude for the people and things you have in your life, a world opens up to you, and a path to happiness opens up a door to you, and life becomes exciting. Gratitude is a habit that frees your soul.

I love the people of the jungle. Their culture is their true wealth. Bartaloy is a mentally challenged man who lives in our village; I believe he's autistic. He slept in the street or the jungle, he couldn't keep himself clean, he had a forty-word vocabulary but always was helpful and kind, so I would give him food, buy him snacks, bread, or bananas.

When I first met Bartaloy, some of the kids in the village had tied a fishing line around his wrist very tightly. I was very angry and yelled at the boys and told one of them to get me a knife, and he helped me remove the string. Bartaloy was very happy to be cut free, and I got him some bread. Marge came and told me his story. He was seven years old and his sister was six when they witnessed their mother getting crushed by a coconut tree during a typhoon, and it affected them both very deeply. Bartaloy evolved toward the jungle, surviving on dead animals and fruit. He would come to the village; his father would try to help him, clean him, feed him, but he would not stay and always go back to the jungle. His sister, Mayong, had many difficulties; she would not stay in school and had many challenges to face, then she met Edwardo and got married.

Bartaloy normally had no sandals; his fingernails always were filthy and encrusted with dirt, and he would wear clothes until there was nothing there, and he would be standing in the street with his dick hanging out, so every two weeks, I would get my brothers-in-law, and we would clean Bartaloy and put fresh clothes on him. I would take a mop and soap him up then hose him down, and my brothers-in-law would change his clothes. Bartaloy always had a big smile on his face, and he would tell the pretty girls, "I love you, *di*." *Di* is short for *indi* that means *girl*. He was kind and played with the other kids in the village. His father and stepmother tried to keep him close to home. Sometimes we would see him hanging out at the bus terminals; they would let him ride because he would help load and unload cargo from the buses, and they would give him food and a few pesos. Sometimes he would be gone for a few months at a time, and there would be sightings in neighboring cities, some as far as four hours by bus away.

In 2007 his stepmother died while pregnant on the way to the hospital in the back of Uncle Larry's truck. She had eight children. She would try to keep Bartaloy cleaned up, but then he would take off and go somewhere, everywhere. In 2009 I was walking through the village, and I saw him. He waved at me from the front of his father's house. No one had seen him. He had been sick, and he died shortly afterward. He was young, early thirties. It may have been TB or an infection. The neighbors collected money to pay for his funeral. Every year there are five to ten funerals, but there are also five to ten new births, and when people die in our village, each house gives twenty pesos to pay for the funeral, and there's normally a seven-day funeral with drinking, bingo, cards, snacks. The gambling raises money for the family of the departed, and the funerals are always held at the house of the departed. Family comes from everywhere, some as far as the States, Australia, Europe, Arab Emirates, and other countries within Asia. Families are genuinely close.

Richy, the village bad boy "The coconut is very quick, and the mountain's covered with blood." Richy is a friend of mine. Sometimes I have to deal with his antics. He likes to get drunk and get wild, and I'm much bigger, and I can grab him by his ankles and hold him upside down till he straightens out. Sometimes I think I'm the only one he respects; he likes to gamble at the cockfights, and his wife gets angry and pinches him. She knows how to deal with him; he is funny and has a great sense of humor, but he has to be watched. One night, Uncle Larry and I got drunk, and Larry wanted to hang out at Richy's uncle's house. We were joking with Richy, but Uncle Larry kept calling Richy a retard, so Larry was very drunk, and he decided to piss down into this ditch, and Larry fell into the ditch with his shorts around his legs, so I had to climb down into the ditch and get Larry's shorts back up. I had to carry Larry home. Marge came along, and after we got him to bed, we raided his refrigerator and ate M&Ms and made popcorn and sang karaoke, and when we were finished, we closed the house and walked down the driveway, and there was Richy, walking down the road. He did not see us. He was talking to himself, saying, "I will show them, I will show them." So we went home; next thing, we heard a commotion, and Richy woke up his uncle and said he was going to burn down the family house and that he should probably get up and get his family out of the house. Uncle Carl convinced him that it was not a good idea and to go home and sleep it off.

Richy is a wild child. He likes to go to the cockfights and gamble. He's a rebel at heart, but you never know how the evening is going to end up, what type of wildness will happen, or if soldiers are going to show up and tell Richy to go home or take him to jail for the night.

Ester and Binarondo love to drink. They weave baskets and make brooms and sell them in the neighboring villages. They never miss a funeral; it's an opportunity to drink. Ester is in her seventies, and Binarando in his early forties. I always see Ester walking down the street with a banana leaf on her head if it's raining or if the sun is out. They bathe in the ocean, and they like to drink root wine, *shauktong*, and they work full-time to keep themselves pickled, then Binarondo dances by the karaoke bar, and the kids laugh and have fun with him. Ester sits and watches, and if any girls come through the village, she raises hell because she thinks every girl is trying to steal her Binarondo away from her. It's an evening of entertainment. Sometimes she gets wild and raises hell with the other girls in the village, but there's always people on the street, neighbors, motorcycles, taxis, and carabaos dragging bamboo or lumber out of the village, people going to the church or prayer meetings at houses, people passing through, and visitors.

A couple of times a month, we lose electricity because of a storm, and sometimes it's for several days, but people still find a way to stay entertained—playing basketball or drinking with the neighbors or just visiting with one another.

CHAPTER 6

M arge and I were engaged, and I was to return to the States for a few months to finish up some loose ends. I was departing Thanksgiving weekend, and I ran into some trouble. You see, before I went to the Philippines, I asked my travel agent if I required a visa, and she asked me, "Are you American?" I said "Yes." She said, "You won't need a visa." I said "Great." So before I went, I gave Marge and her mother what money I had, figuring I'm going back. Now problem when I got to the immigration stand, they said I owed eight thousand pesos. I said, "I don't have it"; they said, "You can't go." I was terrified, so I gathered myself together, and I went to the airlines, explained the situation, and they said they could change my ticket as soon as I got my immigration settled. OK, great, so I called my parents in Florida and explained to them that I was stranded in Manila and I needed some money.

My sister sent a Western Union on her credit card, and I called back and got the numbers. Only it was too late, the last plane had already departed, and it was too late to get a Western Union, so I was talking to the head of security at the airport. He was a kind man, and he said I could stay at his house, so I was talking to the girls at the rent-a-car, and I told them what was going on, and the head of security offered to let me stay with him at his house. They said he was a nice man and that it was a shame what happened to his wife. I said, "What happened?" The girl said, "She was found stabbed to death in their house." At this time he came up to me and asked if I wanted to stay at his house. I said, "No, I want to stay at the airport, but thank you just the same."

The following day was Bonifacio Day, and all the Western Unions were closed, so I slept on filing cabinets at the rent-a-car for two nights before I could get the Western Union to pay the Immigration to leave, so finally I got on a flight to LA. I was so happy. So I was in LA, trying to get on a flight to Florida. Standby it's Thanksgiving. I slept under a park bench for three nights before they could get me on a flight going to North Carolina. They asked me if I would like to sit in first class. I naturally said yes. I smelled so bad after sleeping in airports for five nights. I felt bad for the kind man who sat next to me. I told the flight attendant to keep the rum and Cokes flowing my way; if I'm going to smell bad, I may as well be drunk, and after one more flight, the plane was landing in West Palm Beach. I cried out "Thank God" with tears in my eyes. They must have thought I had a screw loose. I took the taxi to my mother's house, went to the backyard, took off all my clothes and set them on fire on the grill, went into the bathroom, found the clippers under the sink, shaved every hair off my body, and proceeded to shower over an hour and a half. It was truly the toughest trip of my life.

Within my first day of returning, I found out my taxi partner Juan Alonzo was found in his apartment dead of a heart attack. He died a week earlier, and they just found the body. He was on his couch, and the neighbors complained. We worked together at Yellow Cab; he was a supervisor (Safety), a Vietnam veteran, and a close friend to me. It really affected me; we were kindred spirits. He was teaching me Spanish, and sometimes we would have a beer together and talk about God, our lives as taxi drivers, his life in Cuba as a young boy, his days in Vietnam. He will always be remembered.

CHAPTER 7

Driving a taxi in Palm Beach since 1984. Every time I come back from the Philippines, I drive here in West Palm Beach. I haven't used a map in over fifteen years, and the people that I meet have interesting lives, and I get to share my stories and pictures from the jungle, and I tell my customers the story of how my wife and I met and how we wrote letters to each other and how we fell in love from ten thousand miles away through letters and how I went there and married this beautiful native girl and made her my wife. So while I'm driving, so many people have gotten to ride in my taxi and have heard the stories, and most of the time, I get a very feel-good response from my customers, and I have heard for years, "You should write your stories down," "Create a book," or they say, "This is the coolest cab ride I've ever had."

The other taxi drivers put their hopes in me, and many drivers live vicariously through me. It is a taxi driver's dream to lie in a hammock on the beach, drinking rum and Coke with a beautiful girl there beside you on a perfect beach on a perfect night; that is truly magic. And while I'm driving taxi, I will tell my stories of the things I've encountered along the way.

Truth be told, I like to come back to Florida, drive taxis. I always have a great time and meet nice people who have come to Florida on vacation, and sometimes it's a challenge. Normally, I work every day so I can send money home every week to take care of Marge and the kids.

Normally, I drive 120 hours a week, so with that much exposure, things happen—you see accidents and crimes and all sorts of things you wouldn't see in a normal job. I got a call one night to an address on a dead-end street. I honked my horn, but no one came out, so I backed out of the driveway and saw a fat black woman and a ten-year-old boy. I rolled down the passenger window of the taxi and asked where they were going. At the same time, I felt a gun strike my head from the driver's side and a voice saying, "Give me your money, motherfucker." So I responded by grabbing the gun and holding it to the ceiling of the cab, but he wouldn't let go. So I stepped on the gas and dragged him along the side of the car. It was a dead-end street, so I let go of the gun, and he fell in the middle of the street, so I turned around in someone's yard, and he was trying to crawl out of the street, knowing he still had the gun. I aimed the car for him, ducked down into the seat, and hit the gas. He managed to get out of the car's way in time, so I went around the corner, and there was a cop. I told him what happened, so they dispatched cars to try to catch this lowlife. They told me they chased him for a while and he disappeared into the ghetto.

I've had guns pointed at me a few times over the years. It's not a good feeling, and the memory lasts with you a long time. Over the years, I've had people try stupid things in my taxi—attempted robberies or people trying to score drugs or trying to run without paying—but I've got a cure for a bad attitude: pay me and get out. Life is too short to ride around with an asshole in the car.

I think back over the years and remember my friends who have died and my friends who have been murdered driving a taxi in South Florida. I can't remember them all anymore. My buddy Steve was found murdered in the trunk of his taxi in a rural Palm Beach county neighborhood a week after he had been shot to death, or my buddy Garry who was shot in the back of the head and the phone call I made, telling his wife he'd been shot. I sat with his family, and we prayed together at the hospital. And my friend Michael, who owned a neighborhood bar in West Palm Beach, who was murdered by his lover, then his lover took his own life. Michael Brown was a great man who would do anything to help a friend. And back when I had the limousine company, I parked one of my limos at his bar, and whenever Michael needed to go anyplace, he would call me. When I heard he had been killed, I was so angry and at such a loss.

CHAPTER 8

I was driving a taxi in West Palm Beach in 1997 when I passed an old limousine with a For Sale sign. I stopped and took a look at it, a 1986 Lincoln six passenger. It needed a lot of work. He wanted $1,200 for it, but I talked him down to $900 and took the car home. Two weeks went by, and I was driving my taxi, and I saw on the side of the road a limousine for sale, so I stopped and had a look at it—another 1986 Lincoln stretch six passenger. His sign said $1,400 OBO. I had $1,000 on me, so I told him, "This is what I have on me, take it or leave it." He took the money, and I got a twin for my other limo. I drove a taxi, and every chance I had to fix something or replace a part then, I started pulling these old limos apart, taking out all the interior pieces. I made tables out of plywood and sawhorses, went to the fabric store, purchased thirty yards of zebra-print crushed velvet and all the padding adhesive, contact cement, took all these things back to my place, and started rebuilding the limos. I paid a buddy $20 an hour, and we worked around the clock, and we got the limos on the road. We always found a way to make it all happen, so now I had two tripped-out pimp limos.

The cars were fun; we went everywhere—concerts, events. My son Kevin would come for the summers, and I would chauffeur him around in the limos. And I was performing in community theater. Kevin would be backstage with me during rehearsals. I was typecast the duke, doing Shakespeare. We did four plays, so they were long hours of reading and practice, but we would go out and take the limos for the Moonfest parade in West Palm Beach, Florida.

We had some great summers, and we always had a great time.

CHAPTER 9

The hut was a place where artists would rent a small space in a warehouse. There was always a group of people hanging out. The guy who ran the place organized neighborhood events, art shows, played live music. He was a talented middle-aged man, a nonconformist. He had a love for Miller beer and Lucky Strikes; he would repair antique furniture and do refinishing. His work was good, but then he would start with his hippie shmeal, talking about the man and whatever conspiracy was currently going on. I lived in a loft there. There were others who lived there as well as a young born-again Christian guy. He would have Friday Christian coffee night, and he would serve coffee and food he would find in dumpsters to his Christian youth group. And there were two old black men who would hang out by the train tracks and drink beer, Lorenzo and Willy, and they shared a spot and a love for cheap alcohol and pickled pig's feet.

I would sing the blues and play my guitar. I would sing BB King songs and play the dirty low-down blues for them—a Polish couple, a Russian artist, a few Irish artists, a bicycle taxi company, my limousine service, a man who worked on yachts, a nudist couple, a puppet lady who had patches of facial hair, the crackheads and an assortment of freaks, dropouts, ten-time losers, pseudointellectuals, man-hating lesbians, and every other freak under the sun, but the place had an open-door policy, and everyone would show up sooner or later for a party or an event.

The building was an old metal building. The wood was all eaten away by the termites, and the rats and the possums also live there, and when it rained, there was eight inches of water on the floor and electric wires running everywhere. It's a wonder no one was killed.

It was my preamble in moving to the jungle—lots of mosquitoes, termites, stagnant water, and lots of loser fuckwads, drunks, drug addicts, but there were a few people who had their shit together, people who had jobs and lives, who stayed because of cheap rent; the hut attracted certain people who just wanted to hang out because the man who ran the place was always drinking, and he would give the bums beer and cigarettes, but he would help anyone who came through the doors. So there was always something going on, a play or an art showing, live music, life drawing, and there were always spectators. And there were a few of us who truly connected with one another and have remained close over the years. I guess when I think back, the days at the hut were fun, and even when personalities clashed, I will always have a soft spot in my heart for the friends who gathered.

Rooster had a jeep covered in sea glass and seashells and a mannequin head mounted on the hood, and it was decorated in sea glass and seashell, then he covered an RV in sea glass and shells. And he would sell his artwork; he would craft mois (*tiki* heads) out of papier-mâché and wood. His art has sold well over the years, and his boui babies are the rage.

Tom T3 lived in the neighboring bay and drove a bicycle taxi at night downtown, and during the day, he worked on yachts, doing repairs, mechanics, etc. He would help me when I needed the radiator replaced on my limousine, and he would always help me if I was in a spot. Thirteen years later, we are still good friends. There's nothing I wouldn't do for Tom, and there's nothing Tom wouldn't do for me, so we continue doing nothing for each other, to listen to Anthony Robbins CDs, you know, the self-help guru, and I started writing down my plan in great detail, how I wanted to sell the limos and do something else and get out of there.

There was an alliance within the group of people who where there all the time, and we watched out for one another. We would drink together and laugh, smoke, and keep one another sane, but we were always bombarded by crackheads and people who had nowhere else to go.

After living there for two years, I wanted to sell the limousine service and go somewhere. When I was small, I always had a deep fascination with Asian cultures. I wanted to learn karate and be the next Bruce Lee or a shogun warrior, and the women were so attractive and graceful, and the artwork carved dragons and inlaid furniture always profoundly move me, the dedication they put into their art. From a young age, I desired to explore the world, find a beautiful Asian girl to share my life with, so I made a plan in my mind to get some money together and go for it, so I had this small party.

Limousine service makes enough money to escape from America and go to a place that is cheap to live, a place where the girls are beautiful and friendly, a place that I could make my home and simplify my life and raise a family without the distractions and the confusion of living in America, and I found it in the Philippines. The people are kind and generous; there's always laughter in the streets, and there's always people sharing with one another.

CHAPTER 10

The one thing that has stuck with me for the last ten years was the formula to create my lifestyle, and I spent a lot of time on writing down the things I want in great detail—the marriage, the home, the relationships with my children, the way we spend our days together, and the way I want my children to look at life with a healthy attitude so they know that anything is possible, how to set and achieve goals, and that anything is possible and that normally, we don't know how things are going to happen, and that is not our worry. All we have to do is focus on the result and every day to take what steps we can to be closer to our dreams and feel the feelings of already having the things we truly desire, how we will feel once we already have the relationship, the house and children, the money, the lifestyle. All these things find us as we seek them with a healthy attitude.

This book is a dedication to my wife and children. They give me strength and the desire to move mountains, and I know if I teach them to write down the things they want in life, it's the first step in getting what they want. And the more emotional they are about it, the better.

I have great hopes for the future, and I feel that I make a difference in many people's lives. Most people I've asked the question, what will make you happy? Or what's your idea of paradise? Is it the big house, the nice car? For me, my vision is being on a beach with my wife and children and they are happy and healthy, lying in my hammock with a rum and Coke under a Talisay tree. To quote my dear friend Mo, "As long as everyone is happy." Happiness is the most important thing in this life, and it's not overrated, your joy, your gratitude, your life. And at every opportunity to show and feel true gratitude, you open up the possibility of great things happening. This world operates on good energy. Sometimes we have to change our habits. Watching too much news and TV is bad; the time can be better spent focusing on your dreams and how you want to live your days, what kind of relationships you want with the people around you. Once you have chosen this path, you will surround yourself with people who think like you, people who are living deliberately, people who can identify with what will bring true happiness for them. And though it's a different vision for everyone, the process is the same, being able to receive what you ask for and knowing what you want.

CHAPTER 11

We live our lives in the jungle, where we can teach our children a healthy life and the natural order of life, an unspoken code of ethics and morals, a pattern to live our lives in peace and harmony. We celebrate our births as a tribe and mourn deaths as a tribe. We believe in the power of God and accept that there is a natural order. Life is truly a blessing, a discovery of life, love, and gratitude.

We begin by teaching our children bathing and hygiene and, as they get bigger, their laundry, then how to get their food, how to grow it, then we teach them how to clean a chicken, how to pull the feathers, take out the organs, also how to clean a fish, a snake, a pig, and a goat, etc., so that if anything happens to us as parents, our children will know how to survive. We also teach our children to use a *bolo* (machete) at a very young age and a respect to keep their digits intact and are required to take a *bolo* to school to cut the grass in the school yard.

Children here get circumcised at the age of eight, and to them this is a rite of passage to manhood, and the boys look forward to their circumcision. Children in the jungle mature quicker than kids in Western cultures because more responsibility is required to survive in the jungle, so at a young age, like two or three, they have to go to the store for laundry soap or bleach, vinegar, soy sauce, etc., ask for what is needed and pay for it, and bring back the change. Children are also required to be respectful at all times, no exceptions.

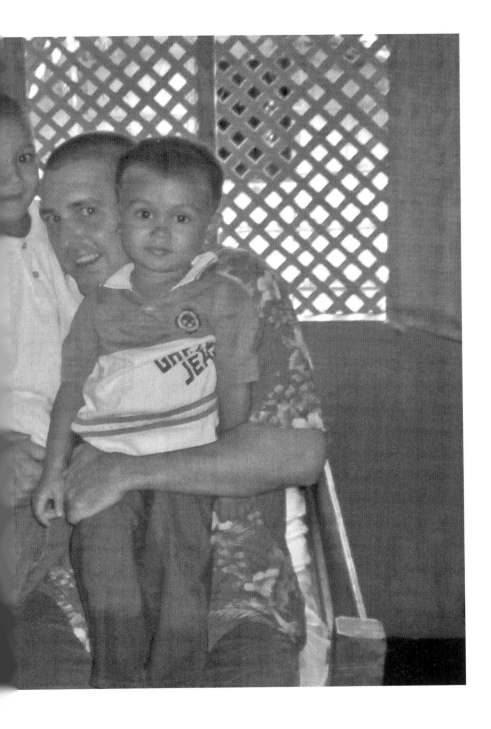

Kevin is my oldest son. He was born at St. Mary's Hospital in West Palm Beach, Florida, in 1992. When he turned one, we moved to Germany, and his mother and I worked for the US military. After five years, his mother and I separated, and Kevin and I returned to South Florida. He told me he missed his mother, and I didn't want to be bitter and keep him away from her, so I sent him back to Germany to be with his mother. He attended school at Ramstein Air Base.

I've always regretted making that choice and always knew in my heart that Kevin would have been much better off with me, so I moved to London, England, and made arrangements with his mother to bring him.

It was great. We went everywhere, rode the subway, played music at the King's Cross subway station, or we would go to Lesture Square. I would give him a harmonica and play the guitar, and the people would clap and toss money. He's a star. I heard people say he was a cute child.

Then I remarried in the Philippines, and my second son was born on the same day as Kevin, so I named him Keith. He was born in 2004, then the following year, Kyle was born 2005, then in 2009, Kenny was born. Kevin has not met with his brothers yet, but Keith, Kyle, and Kenny talk about their big brother in America. Kevin's their hero; they are so proud of him and want him to come and stay, and though this would be a huge deal for me, Kevin's a young man trying to find a job and discovering who he is along the way. My goal is to bring my children together.

While the world is an ever-changing place, I feel it's my responsibility to provide my children with the tools they will need for the future. The world is a changing place, and the way things were done in the past is not the way things will be done in the future. And the most important things to teach our children are how to plant food, how to catch fish and live off the land, how to plant trees and create the life that will bring them true happiness.

Being happy is the most important thing in life. My son Kevin is a great example of a young man living out his dreams, and my job as his father is to give him encouragement at ever becon opportunity. I tell him take chances and pursue his dreams with passion to build the road map to his paradise.

CHAPTER 12

M arge and I would write letters back and forth; she won my heart. She is a great person, and I pray that she is always by my side. She has taken care of me. She is everything in my world. She is a divine spirit, and I proudly call her my wife. She has done so much for me. She heals my soul, she makes me want to be a better man, she always comes to my side in my hour of need. I believe in her. She's the mother of my babies. As the years roll on, I love her more and more. She's my lady of the islands. I plant my faith with her, and she helps me move mountains. She is an inspiration to me and everyone she meets. Her heart is pure, and her spirit is enchanting, and her love for me and my children is something I will always treasure. She is the inspiration behind me. Her letters always had lipstick kisses. I would douse my letters with a nice cologne. The letters took on an average of three weeks for hers and for mine, so a certain degree of patience and anticipation. Her words and thoughts and her natural sincerity, her thoughtful words were always well received. The journey was sacred; it was a commitment to each other and the faith in her that I would always come home to her, a commitment and a promise I look forward to keeping.

And we joke about our children one day giving us grandchildren and the grandchildren have to come up the mountain to visit grandma and grandpa. We see ourselves growing old together there. I remind Marge that I want to be buried on top of my mountain and have my loved ones there beside me, my sons, my wife, my legacy.

CHAPTER 13

The woven bamboo walls and the rattan hammocks, couches, and chairs made of bamboo, the hand-carved drums, and the wall decorations from Bali create a flow of energy, and the wind comes in off the bay, a form of true perfection, a place where my thoughts have manifested like colors to a canvas. I have always had a clear understanding of what paradise is for me; it's living in a place of harmony with my wife and children, a place I call paradise, with all the challenges. I would not change a thing.

It's so nice to go home to the house my wife and I built together, overlooking the bay at the end of the valley. It's my home in the jungle. It's nice to drink young coconut water or cut a ripe pineapple (*pinnia*) or jackfruit (*nunka*). We have a sander fruit (*santol*) and coco trees, mango trees, plum trees (*lumeboy*), papaya trees, banana and plantain trees (*saging*), and many hardwood trees, most being red mahogany. And every year we plant more as the budget allows for posterity's sake, my children and grandchildren. This is a lesson all good men should teach their children. And there's a great wealth in this knowledge—to stay abundant, plant trees.

I love the waterfalls of Pancil. It's a magical place where you can cool off on a hot day and relax and have a beer with an old friend. The water has carved pools in a huge rock. There are many springs through the mountains and a great place to go and explore. You can always find a guava along the trail in a cool place.

Pancil is a property I got after I had been living in the Philippines for over a year. It's a mountain that has waterfalls that run year round. The people are kind and simple; they love to drink the coconut wine. It stains their teeth red. Most people like to sing karaoke in the jungle.

Pancil is a jungle mountain village. The people are tough, and they carry swords. Most go to church and have a lot of faith in the spirit world and a close bond with neighbors and family. I built a cabin there six years ago, and over the last two years, I've built a house at the top of the mountain, and I've put people to work on the construction of the place. The walls are woven bamboo, and the wood is red mahogany. The house overlooks Sogod Bay in Southern Leyte. I like to call it my pirate house. The hammocks are rattan, and the furniture is all bamboo. This is a vision of paradise—a big tropical drink in your hands, a view of Sogod Bay. It's truly a mountain cathedral. It's a very majestic place, and the people are wonderful. I've had the good fortune of making this place my home. My children love Pancil; they enjoy the waterfalls, and they always have a great time. You can feel the natural harmony from the ocean to the jungle. It's captivating and refreshing, and it's the place I feel the most alive. It's been a project I've put my thoughts and passion into the place. There are thousands of pineapples on the property and lots of trees. The neighbors are very helpful. My place is tucked back into the mountains. I like the privacy, and it's a peaceful atmosphere. I wanted to make a place that would feel native for the people who come to visit so they might have the full-on island experience, a place where you can let your hair down and be a pirate. It's a lot of fun and romantic for couples, and it's a great adventure if you're on your own. And there's no shortage of beautiful girls, and you will meet someone special and have the time of your life.

Pancil is romantic. The waterfalls are a great place to take someone you have feelings for. The night skies are always so filled with stars without the distraction of city lights; the stars feel so much closer, and the moon reflects on the bay, and all the fishing boats with their lanterns burning look like fireflies on the water, and the silhouette of the mountains on the other side of the bay through the starlit night.

My mountain house faces the east with a consistent breeze that comes off the bay; this, in my eyes, is paradise.

The story of Robinson Crusoe has always had a profound effect on me. His adventures and the thought of starting a new life on a foreign shore, a tropical paradise where beautiful island girls seek you out and desire you, what's not to love? And going out to a restaurant costs three to five dollars, renting a cabin on the beach for twelve to fifteen dollars with great accommodation or going diving in one of the best spots in the world. There are 7,106 Islands, so you can always catch a boat going somewhere, but I will be on my farm, planting trees, watching my children growing up in the house we built, eating off the farm we planted in Pancil.

CHAPTER 14

I'm always going back to the jungle, and when I'm there, I get up by the second crowing of the rooster that is 4:00 a.m. I like the early morning sky; it gives me a tranquil feeling as I set out on my kitchen steps and smoke a cigarette, catching the first glimpse of the sun, and usually, one or two of the children are awake, so I make us all a cup of chocolate and some bread (*pan*), *hoppia*, and the native coco *siquoti*.

Marge likes to sleep in unless it's Sunday, and we go to church early in Malitbog Santo Niño Parish. I can only last so long, Marge, because the benches are hard, and it hurts my back, so I walk through the plaza across the street and sit beneath these huge trees that were planted by a monk five or six hundred years ago.

The trees are huge and were planted in an orderly fashion. The people of Malitbog hold their festivals, coronations, pageants, and Sinulog Festival, the cultural native festival with lots of dancing and pageantry, in the beginning of December. It's a lot of fun, and everyone gets involved.

On Friday nights some of the Ex-pats get together for drinks usually in Padre Borgos at one of the many Kareoke bars on the bay or dive resorts its a pleasant get together always different people out for drinks

CHAPTER 15

We met Bruno and Daday at a mutual friend's birthday party. We sat next to one another in lawn chairs on the Bermuda lawn and instantly were kindred spirits. Over the past eight and a half years, we have helped each other, and we have built our places. Bruno and Daday have built their beach resort and restaurant while Marge and I have built our place in the mountains. Together we have made our plans and invested ourselves in a future, in a place so distant and far away. When my youngest son was born, we asked them if they would be the godparents, and they accepted. So they attended our fiesta in Sangahon, and we made disco disco, and we got drunk (*hobog*) and danced with our ladies until 4:00 a.m., and they had to be back at 9:00 a.m. for the baptism. I roasted a pig that morning for the celebration, and we drank more beer until we felt better. We served the pig. The skin was nice and crispy, and Marge and Daday each ate a pig ear, pots and pots of food, fish for the people with high blood, and people were in and out of the house, drinking and eating, celebrating and toasting the baptism of my youngest son, Kenny Martin.

Marge and I stay close to home with the kids. We have lots of fun just taking them to the beach or the farm. If we go do something, it's with our friends. We have many things in common, our ages and that we've created a life as foreigners in the jungle, and we have a vision of what we want for ourselves. We have this in common.

It's also a chance to get out and drink beers at the karaoke bars and the dive resorts. I like to take my wife to Cantamuac to visit with our friends Bruno and Daday. They have a beach resort, Southern Leyte Cottages, and they have cabins on the beach for $15 a night, and the restaurant is, in my opinion, the best that Southern Leyte has to offer. It's so beautiful there. It takes your breath away, and they are such good people and dear friends of Marge and me. We have had one great time after another, and I treasure knowing them. We always have great adventures together riding motorcycles, exploring the jungle, or going to the waterfalls. There is a lot to go see—fiestas, discos, coronations—and the food is wonderful, and the girls are so kind and beautiful.

We have the most beautiful girls in the world. More Filipinas have won Miss Universe than any other country. It's a cheap place to live and a cheap place to visit, and when you come, you're treated wonderfully. And it's such fun to ride on the motorcycle taxis and the jeepneys, and it's always very cheap. I get around by motorcycle and put the wife and kids on the bike, and that's how we roll. It's good and healthy for the kids to ride, and to feel the freedom is the best thing for the brain.

Uncle Larry, my grandmother's youngest brother, is a man who could never pass up a challenge. When I was a child, I heard the stories of Uncle Kenny, Merit, Larry, and Uncle Kenny Rosenbrook, a.k.a. Uncle Fuzzy, who served as a seabee during WWII, who had a great influence on my youth.

My mother would take us to visit on weekends to Verni and Fuzzy's house. I would bring my saxophone and play for him what I had learned in school, and he would always ask me, "Can you play 'Far Away'?" And I would always say, "I don't know that song." He would share with me his stories during the war, and when I turned sixteen years old, he gave me his motorcycle.

It was a Honda 350, and it was nice. Uncle Fuzzy had emphysema, and his condition was severe. He was bedridden and on a ventilator, but his eyes would light up when I would come for visits. And he would struggle to speak, so I would do most of the talking. To me he was larger than life even though his physical condition was poor. His character would pour through his piercing green eyes. He was a man's man, a hero, an icon of his time, and his brothers-in-law, who all served during the war—my uncles Kenny, Merit, Larry—they came home and started their lives, got married, and went to work, had their children, built their houses, and liked to play wild.

Merit and Larry were close. Merrit served in the navy, and Larry was first airborne during the fifties. They relocated to Florida to start new lives and open a skydiving club. Then the tragic skydiving accident that took my Uncle Merit's life in 1957, ten years after all three brothers returned from the war. Merit and Larry where living just north of Tampa, and they opened the first private jump club. They both had wives and children. Larry had decided not to go diving that day, but Merit wanted to jump. He invited his wife and three young children to watch. Merrit loved the rush of jumping and enjoyed the free fall, and he had opened his chute a few seconds too late. The family was traumatized; at the last minute, Larry decided to go on the way to the jump site. Merrit's wife and his three young children were traumatized in the car after watching their father fall to his death. So Larry drove down to the site where he saw the parachute spread out in a perfect circle over the body. He pulled the chute back and saw his brother's broken-up body. The years that followed were very difficult for Larry. He lived in several different countries and married three times and fathered seven children. He was a draftsman/engineer for many years and has resided in Sangahon, Malitbog, Southern Leyte, Philippines, for the last sixteen years with his wife, Flor.

They have a home and a small coconut plantation and a home in Seattle, Washington. He's a good-hearted man who loves his wife, and he's my drinking partner in the Philippines. He likes the ladies and loves to flirt with the young girls. He sings karaoke, always the same songs—"Blue Eyes," "Crying in the Rain," "Only You," "Jambalaya," "Delilah"—over beer or Tanduay Rhum. Over the past eight years, I've gotten to know and bond with my Uncle Larry.

Uncle Larry is very good to the people of Sangahon. At Christmas, Larry and Flor give to every house in the village rice, towels, sardines, canned food, soap, etc., and they throw a big party for all the neighbors with games and giveaways, gifts, and always lots of food and drinks. And most of the foreigners come and visit, and there's always a roasted pig, fried chicken, and lots of candy and ice cream for the kids. His wife is a wonderful cook and a great hostess. She makes everyone feel at home and welcome. Everyone has a great time, and there's a lot of drinking and games for the kids, and everyone has fun.

Now in 2010, Larry and his sister Verni are the last remaining of my grandmother's generation, a generation that survived a war and great personal losses. I want to honor them in the making of this book about my family for posterity's sake, for my children and grandchildren. I owe a debt of gratitude to my Uncle Larry for all the great times, for the wild nights of fun, and for opening his heart and sharing with me in good times and bad times. We are kindred spirits.

In 2001 I wrote him an e-mail, telling him I wanted to meet a nice Filipina girl. His wife replied to my e-mail. She told me she had a few friends. A month later, I got a letter in the mail from a girl named Marge Cabel. She told me she was twenty-one and that she wanted to meet a nice American man. The letter was so captivating, and the broken English gave the letter a sense of mystery, so I responded, and we had a dialogue for a year that enticed me to buy a plane ticket and travel to the Philippines to meet her. Her humble and sweet personality won my heart. Her attitude was a breath of fresh air, and when I met her, she was just as kind and sincere as her letters revealed her to be.

And wow, her beautiful face and healthy young body made me go wild from the moment I saw her that first day when I came to the village. I knew this was the girl for me. She won my heart, and as the days followed, it was incredible. This native island girl rescued me from myself.

CHAPTER 16

The island calls to my spirit. In fact, the word *malitbog,* "of the spirit," has a history rich in tradition. In the third week of January, we have Sinulog festival, a cultural celebration of native dress and dance, and the villages all come out to compete for best costume, best dance, and everyone gets involved, from the very young to the very old. The colors are vibrant, and a passion flows through the streets, a love for their heritage, a love for their country. I feel truly honored to be a part of the community.

The dresses and the costumes are so creatively designed, and the colors are always breathtaking. There's a ferris wheel they set up every year and booths with games and prizes and a bingo booth. Food and drink are sold by street vendors, lots of booths to buy toys and sunglasses, earrings, necklaces, popcorn, peanuts, cotton candy. The people are very proud of their culture, and Magellan's mass is reenacted. Also Magellan and Lapu-Lapu, the famous Filipino chieftain whose soldiers killed Magellan in Mactan Island in 1621. Each age group has teams. They divide up into tribes and do their show, and the tribes are judged on their dance, costumes, original concepts. There are always lots of chicken feathers, and everyone always has a great time. The men are dressed as warriors, and the girls are all native princesses, and the dancing and singing goes on for a few days, and everyone always gets involved in the parades. It's a great thing, an awesome experience, a memory for a lifetime.

Cebu

Ninoy Aquino International Airport in Mactan Island. Cebu is a place with so many things to see. Santo Niño Church is a must-see; it's awesome, a beautiful masterpiece, an inspiration of God. You wait in a line in the courtyard to visit the shrine and say a prayer and touch the glass of Santo Niño. Thousands go daily.

Cebu is a crowded place with lots to see and do. Cebu has great malls, affordable hotels, great dining, and lots to explore and see. But caution: this is not a place to break the law or act out. Being a foreigner, the eyes are on you, so act accordingly. Most people live very conservatively, and they frown on Western arrogance. It's very important to be respectful at all times; remember, you're the visitor. Most places are safe to roam while other places require being aware of your surroundings. My favorite thing to do in Cebu is to shop for pearls on the streets or in the market. The deals you can find are unreal, but be careful; the best market for finding pearls is the Carbon market. Caution: there are lots of pickpockets.

Do not give beggars money. It's an ignorant thing to do. You show them where you keep your money, and they will rob you blind. Keep your money, put it away, and don't let people get close to you, especially children. The old saying goes "A fool and his money shall soon part." Don't let people close to you, tell the children not to bother you, be loud if you have to, and never pull out all your money on the streets. Just keep a few pesos in your pocket at a time—two hundred to five hundred pesos. That's more than enough to have readily available. You will find great deals and nice artworks.

There's a restaurant I like to go to in Cebu. It's on Mango road, the Lighthouse Restaurant; I love this place. The food is great. We always get lobster dinners, calamari, drinks, dessert, and the place is nice. At the end of the night, our bill is normally ten to twelve dollars, and the experience is always great and well worth it.

When I'm in Cebu, I always visit my sister-in-law's house. Her name is Marlo, and her husband is Pigeon. They have seven children, so when I come, visit I always bring candy for the kids, and I buy food for the family. The area they live in is Talisay. It's a squatters area, and so I'm always surrounded by kids asking questions about America. It's a difficult place for a foreigner to go; the poverty, the stagnant water, the conditions are very tough, people are kind and happy you came to visit, and you're greeted with open arms everywhere you go.

The hospitality is the best in the world, and you will bond with people, and the children don't act like American children. They have manners and respect. And the streets at night are full of great food, vendors, pork barbecue, chicken, grilled sea food; there's always karaoke, shopping.

The boat ride to Cebu is five hours from Southern Leyte. The ferry boats are covered with pipe-framed bunk beds on all the levels of the boat, so it's a good idea to think of your own safety and stay deck side or hire, so if you have to jump off the boats in an emergency, you will have a better chance to survive. You should always be prepared for whatever may happen. There are potholes in the road, there are unsafe modes of transportation, and sometimes you just have to hold on. Don't overreact to what is going on, and remember, people live this way every day. Babies ride on motorcycles without helmets. Sometimes you're riding a motorcycle with six other people, sometimes you're packed in the back of a bus, but this is part of the adventure; don't miss the forest for the trees. People always make a way for each other. There's always space for one more; there's always enough for everyone. Filipinos are generous people, and they are very caring. They will always share with you even if they only have a little.

MANILA

Manila is a great place, lots of beautiful girls, clubs, shopping, hotels, and lots of great places to eat. Makati is a nice area to visit, and there's lots of malls and markets. You can find bargains and have a great experience, and the nightlife is spectacular. You can spend a few dollars and have a wild experience, but it's good to take a moment to remember that you're visiting, so be smart; don't do anything to get yourself in trouble. Mind your manners, be respectful, and you will be treated respectfully.

My favorite place in Manila is Ermita, also known as Adreatico. There's a nice mall there, Robinsons Mall. It's huge with lots of shops, restaurants, clubs, and the Ermeta Coliseum. They often have concerts like America or Spiral Staircase, Petula Clark, lots of acts from the seventies era, and there are dinner theaters and many shows to go and have fun. Everything is cheaper than what you're accustomed to paying anywhere else.

The most common question I get is "Is it safe?" My answer is yes, it's safe. I've never had a problem. I drink when I get there to help with the jet lag, and I walk down Manila Bay at 3:00 to 5:00 a.m., and I've never had a problem. In fact, I've met wonderful people in my journeys; most of the people you meet over there are good-hearted people who mean you no harm.

The city has a heartbeat. People are going places, doing their thing. You know the song "Manila"? I like to stay in a few different places. You have to find what fits you. There are $1000 hotels, and there are $5 hotels.

Manila has many markets, and there are always things to do. It's a great place. My favorite hotel to stay at is Las Palmas on North Mabini Street. It's next to Robinsons Mall. The rooms' average price is fifty to sixty dollars a night. It's very clean. Casino Filipino is across the street. 7-Eleven is around the corner. There's always someone on the street trying to sell you something—pearls, Viagra, fake Rolex.

Sometimes you can get good deals. Always be careful about pulling out money in front of people and the guys selling pesos on the street. Always exchange money only at hotels or banks, and count your money carefully. I've stayed at nice places, and I've also stayed in some bad places. Generally, you get what you pay for. And I've stayed at some of what I like to call suicide hotels. I've written some of my best poetry in those places, walls stained nicotine yellow, and if there's a knock on your door, don't open the door, or a scream in the hallway, don't open the door. Just like in any big city, you have to be smart. Stupid people find trouble. If you come to the Philippines, always carry hand sanitizer. And keep your money well stashed, and only have in your pocket what you want to spend for the day.

CHAPTER 17

EXPATRIATES

Most of the expats know one another. We get together for birthday parties or the Friday night drinking in Padre Burgos and getting wild. Most of the people you meet are good, and there are all kinds of people. You have to be smart. As far as the people you meet anywhere, most of the expat communities help one another. I owe them a deep debt of gratitude. It takes a certain personality to move into the jungle and be able to survive and do well and plan a future, plant the seeds.

Though this life isn't for everyone, we who have chosen it have a respect and a bond of friendship. We have had many great evenings of laughter and drinking out on the bay. We live in a place that is so beautiful and so majestic. The people are kind, and the girls are so beautiful, and they don't have bad attitudes, and they like to flirt, and they care how they look, and most watch their weight, and they have good manners. That's why foreigners are attracted to the girls, that's why most expatriates live there, because of the aggravation of trying to find an attractive partner without all of the headaches that come with getting involved with a girl from a Western culture.

The ocean, the 7,106 islands, the bamboo huts, and the many modes of transportation create an environment of adventure. Hopping on boats and skipping on different islands is fun. Hotels and cabins on the beaches for three to thirty dollars a night in the province. Buses, boats, and motorcycle taxis.

There are pretty girls everywhere, and there are waterfalls to go visit, mountains to hike, and great diving. But for me, when I go home, the time I spend with my wife is magical. We ride my bike up the bay, and we're always out in the jungle looking for more farmland or taking the kids for a motorcycle ride to the beach or the waterfalls. And the night sky over the bay, the stars (*bituon*), the moon (*buon*), the fishermen in their boats (*sokajan*) with their lanterns lighting up the bay like fireflies, lots of street-side barbecue stands to visit. Sometimes we go to Herman's Karaoke Bar, the Golden Dwarf, or Taundua Daves for an evening of karaoke, and there are usually expats drinking and having a good time out on the bay. People say hello as they go by. It's a retired man's dream.

The Philippines and the people are helpful and thoughtful; that's why foreigners love these shores. It's much better for a foreigner on a fixed income, and for a few dollars you can hire a private nurse and maids, and it's very commonplace to see older white men with native girls.

There's a wide background of expats from many different countries and different careers: retired military, retired prison guards, beer truck drivers, chefs, engineers, roughnecks from every corner of the world. There are so many reasons for being there. It just clearly outweighs the reasons to be anywhere else in the world. Good friends, the cost of living, the relaxed atmosphere, beautiful girls in a place that's not been tainted by technology and the newest trends, it's pure and simple living.

CHAPTER 18

The freedom I feel when I'm there with the people I love is immeasurable. Sure there're not many conveniences, like fast food or easy bathrooms to use, but I'm relaxed there; and I don't stress about the same things I stress about in the States. My life is peaceful and practical—the simple life, the tropical island dream, hammocks, sandals, a bottle of rum, beautiful native girls, pork on the barbecue, long motorcycle rides, gatherings of old friends in a sacred spot (a place you have to visit), have the romance that's the experience of a lifetime, best diving in the world in a place that has such a incredible energy, and where the mountains meet the ocean. Come for the experience, take a leap into a world where people are honorable and have heart and character you can't help but connect with. People have fun; people welcome you in and treat you like family. The locals are kind and giving, the weather is great though it can get very hot. Sometimes it can rain for months at a time as well. The days are so relaxed, and in the village, massages are available for two dollars and manicures and pedicures for a dollar. In dinnertime, we have fish or chicken with rice and vegetables or *pancit* noodles with vegetables and meat. In the city, there're always lots of food venders, and the food is great—everything from grilled fish, roasted chicken, or pork for two dollars. I can buy enough barbecue to feed my family. There's always a pot of rice at our house, so we get the barbecue to go. And we love the motorcycle ride; it's a thrill to be riding through the night sky on the bay with my Marge behind, ready for an evening's adventure. The freedom of being able to step away from all the bullshit, the bad attitudes, the angry people, the imprisoning lifestyle of trying to keep one's head above water with rent payments, insurance payments, credit cards, etc. No cell phones, no nonsense, no TV, no Fox News trying to make this world a scarier place than it already is. If you want to improve your life, turn off the TV; it will have a positive effect on you. And go travel, take chances, learn new languages, meet great people, get a life that doesn't center around totally useless crap, take a healthy step away from the nonsense, break a few patterns, and go for it. Don't sit around and become a useless fat glob of crap; live your dreams now, take action now, take a step toward what is healthy.

As the days go by and I'm here in America, I miss my home and children and my wife, Marge. She is waiting for me to finish this book so I can come home safe to her. She calls me on the phone and tells me the details of my children's lives and their day-to-day events. And this fuels my actions and keeps me sane. She restores my soul, she motivates me, she immortalizes me before my sons; to them, I'm a hero. Her gratitude overflows, and she reminds me of the home we built together, the life we built together, and the love we share that keeps me motivated. She is a good woman, she makes the sacrifices with me, she takes the kids to church, she keeps their heads focused in the right direction. I know from watching her that she's a divine spirit. And I'm so lucky to have her; American woman don't have selfless attitudes and They also have an attitude of entitlement, when there're so many beautiful girls around the world that have not been spoiled and that have not been overindulged. And the men in American culture are so willing to put on a dress and it's a sickness, a weakness of character, and a codependent way of existing. And somehow within American culture, this has become an acceptable way of life. At the end of the day, men give up any pride they have in themselves, and they don't even like who they have become. There was a time when men were men in our culture, And the example that mothers and fathers set for their children is warped and not clear, so we suffer the consequences of yielding and not standing strong in the values they believe and know to be true and correct and healthy. I believe in the life I've created for myself and my family; I've found a inner peace and there's no confusion about our roles as parents and as husband and wife. She cares for our children's direction of their development and their day-to-day needs; I'm the provider of money and food. Time tells the story of who chose the correct path by how children are developed and what kind of people they become and how well they take care of themselves and how they mature, how they react when things get rough, and how well they adapt to complicated situations. It's not the good times that define our character, it's the bad times and how gracefully we adapt and, in the mist of conflict and chaos, how well we create a vision and a path. The heart knows; it's funny how much you can miss someone and try to stay functional and keep it together and not fall to pieces knowing there're ten thousand miles that separate you, but I know that my time here doesn't go in vain, that what money I do get helps my children and my wife, and it makes such a difference in their lives. To see their faces again will put me on cloud nine. I can dream of that day when I take that journey and that twenty-two-hour flight. It is a big deal just to hold them and kiss my wife and hold my babies again, visit my neighbors and loved ones. Their love has held me together emotionally. Crossing to the other side of the world, leaving civilization and the fast food, twenty-four-hour convenience, air-conditioning, and all the things that make American life what it is back to the land of scorpions, monkeys, anacondas, poisonous bugs, centipedes, mountain lice, and all the other distractions that make the jungle what it is; it's my home, it's where I've invested my emotions. And to the people of the jungle, I'm a hero; to the people here in South Florida, I'm a taxi driver, a servant to the people. My mountain is a dream to me; it's the place where my dreams wander, a place where I can let my imagination take me to a simple place, a simple life without all the confusion, a place where I can truly dream and watch my kids grow, eat pineapples out of my fields, or drink coconut water on a hot day and feel the rhythms of the jungle, visit the friends I've grown close to, the life I've embraced that is so completely opposite of the way I grew up, so different from the things I was familiar with in my youth. There's power in knowing what makes you happy; all the answers to my prayers are there, the love I always looked for is there, and I see it when I look into my wife's eyes. She makes my heart beat wildly, her simple grace and beauty is so awesome, she takes me to a place where I'm truly content, and the days are so precious and each kiss takes my heart to a greater place. I'm so glad I took the chance, and I made the journey to be with her; we have built a life together. Our children are strong and smart, we have a clear understanding of our roles as parents and as husband and wife.

A LETTER FROM DAD

Dear Kevin, Keith, Kyle, and Kenny,

The most important thing in this life is to have a clear understanding of what will make you happy, that life is an ever-changing thing, and what's important to you now will change—your priorities, your habits, the way you want your children to see you, and what values you want to share with your children. For me, this is a driving force, and I want to raise my children in a healthy place with healthy habits. I want them to strive for success in whatever they choose for themselves and give them direction and support so they can live a happy life; a person is only as successful as how well they adjust to their surroundings. To be a conscious spirit on the face of the earth with all the possibilities and now with the knowledge of a civilization at our finger tips (Internet), we have the tools to shape our destiny, our path, our children's path, to create the kind of world we want to live in, a world of peace, a world that's not in conflict with itself. And it's up to us to do this, and from what I've learned in the course of my lifetime, every action under the sun has a reaction; and it starts by each of us taking a conscious step every day toward being the person we really want to be. You can choose to live in conflict with your neighbors, your colleagues at work, cars in traffic, or whatever; you will always have issues. But if you take the time to address these issues and always inject good feelings in everything you do, doors will open to you and what seemed impossible becomes the possible. It starts when you are truly grateful, not just the words, it's the emotion of gratitude—that's what shapes your life and brings the people, the travel, the money, all the abundance into your life, all the wonder, all the adventure, all the love. There's a big world out there, and the possibilities are truly infinite; and life is good, and all the blessings are yours for the taking. This book is for you, Live deliberately; don't listen to naysayers and never believe anyone that tells you that anything is impossible. They are not your friends. Believe in your dreams no matter what, and seek out your happiness in all that you do. You will encounter obstacles in this life; take the time to recognize that your thoughts and emotions are always parallel with each other, and your happiness will come from your thoughts and living your dreams.

The world will open up to you, you will be happy and healthy, and you will inspire and move mountains. The real story of my life has always been centered around you, my sons, my four boys: Kevin, Keith, Kyle, and Kenny—my four kings. I've built our family home in a place where water flows through the mountains. I've planted thousands of trees in a place where you can always come home to. The mountain in Sangahon and the mountain in Pancil are yours to farm and protect, and my hopes for the future is that you will have the same love and passion for these mountains as I do. It's the place I built for you to come home to; it's the land of your heritage, and you're my hopes and my prayers for the future. And you will play a great role in making this world a better place, and your children will inherit the seeds you sow. So seize the day; live, love, and find the things that are worthy of you and recognize that no matter what the outcome, that life continues. And you should always move forward and take the time to smell the roses and remember all the wonderful things in this life and what your grateful for—your family, your friends, the clothes you wear, the things you have, the life you've been given, the things you've earned on your own, your abilities. You see, there're a lot to be grateful for, and most of all, be grateful that you have one another. It's where your true strength lies. As I've come to middle age with a degree of grace with a love for my sons, I dream of the day when my oldest son will come and meet his brothers and get to know each other and bond and see all the similarities you have as brothers, all the things you have in common; you're a band of brothers. My love for you all is unmeasurable and eternal. I hope your life is wonderful as my life has been. I love you always, and I'm grateful for being your father. I'm so proud of all four of you, and these words will be eternally in print for you and your grandchildren.

Your father,

Neil A. Hoag

"Hinumdumi ako kanunay" (Remember me always).

ACKNOWLEDGEMENTS

This book was made possible with the help of many good friends—Ken, JC, Brad, Tom and Tyra Cliff, Eddy, Gary, and I can't forget Mo who hired me as a taxi driver when I was a teenager—twenty-five years later we're still hanging at the Dunkin' Donuts on Dixie—and to all the friends who have supported me.

All these years, I love you guys. You make Florida a better place, and my house is always open to you, and I do hope you make the trip and create your own adventure and see why I fell in love.

Made in the USA
Middletown, DE
04 July 2015